Enjoy Your Garden

ROSES
IN COLOUR

Edited by
Michael Gibson

ORBIS PUBLISHING·LONDON

Contents

3 Foreword
5 The rose in religion and symbolism
7 The principal wild roses
8 The development of the garden rose
10 The largest and the smallest rose
11 The rose in the garden
11 Famous rose garden
12 How to grow roses
13 Pests and diseases
13 Pruning
14 The rose in the life of man
14 Recommended roses listed by colour
17 Illustrations

Picture credits: Gregory's Roses, Nottingham: cover; Archivo B, Milan: 38, 40; Armstrong Nurseries, California (photos, C. Bryant): 28, 83; Conard-Pyle Co, Pennsylvania: 77; Fratelli Ingegnoli, Milan: 9, 25, 29, 47, 57, 73, 74, 89, 94, 105, 106, 108; Germain's Inc, California: 27; Michael Gibson: 5, 26, 102, 104; Gregory's Roses, Nottingham: 10–24, 30–37, 44–46, 50–56, 59, 62–70, 72, 75, 76, 78–80, 97, 98, 100, 101, 103; Kayebon Press Ltd, Cheshire: 7, 39, 41, 58, 81, 84–87, 90–92, 95, 96; G. Mazza, Milan: 1; S. McGredy Roses, Portadown (photos, Kayebon Press): 42, 43, 48, 60, 61, 82, 88, 93, 99, 107; SEF, Turin: 2; G. Tomsich, Rome: 3, 4, 49, 71.
Drawings on page 12, 13 and 14 are reproduced from *Roses* by Peter Coats (Weidenfeld & Nicholson).

Adapted from the Italian of Claudia Binelli
Edited by Michael Gibson

Printed in Italy by IGDA, Novara

SBN 0 85613 177 6

Another book on roses? Any rose-lover who sees a new publication on sale may be inclined to wonder how it can possibly be justified. At first glance you might think there was nothing new to be said, no new problem to be studied, so fully have roses been dealt with by distinguished botanists and artists. But if you consider that about twenty-thousand varieties are being cultivated today, and two hundred new varieties are shown at international competitions every year, if you think of their commercial importance, of the thousands of acres on which they are grown all over the world, of their beauty both out of doors and in the house, it becomes clear that there is plenty more to be said about them.

This book deals first of all with the remarkable history of the rose from ancient times until our own day, and with what it has symbolized in the history of man.

There are descriptions of wild species that may still be found in the hedgerows, wild species that are the ancestors of many varieties of cultivated roses.

The development of the cultivated rose is another fascinating subject. Imaginative growers have, down the years, managed to obtain a very wide range of colour, and today by the skilful crossing of roses they are still patiently trying to produce a black or a blue rose.

Then, all down the centuries, both the flower and the fruit of the roses have had various uses, and today they are still used in the making of scents and cosmetics and medicinal products. Roses are commercially important as well, of course, as cut flowers, potted plants, and for display in the garden or in the house. Anyone wanting to grow roses in his garden or on a balcony in town will find in this book advice on how to do so and information about the diseases from which they may suffer.

There are many illustrations, with very full captions, describing many of the best-known modern roses.

The rose needs no recommendation: its fresh, abundant petals, its superb colour, its delicate scent and exquisite form all make it a truly regal flower. Every garden, however modest, needs to have roses in it. In fact, it is impossible to imagine the world without the rose, for it has been adorning the earth since time immemorial, and often serving as a symbol of some aspect of man's history.

'The man with a rose in his hat', says a Mexican proverb, 'has the whole world'—because he has known the beauty of creation and is happy.

Rosa gallica

Published by Dr. Woodville. May 1. 1792.

The rose in religion and symbolism

From the earth's earliest days until the time of Christ, from the Middle Ages until our own day, the rose has been part of man's life on earth, and its origins are lost in legend and in mythology. It is thought possible that it originated in central Asia, spreading eastwards to North America, and westwards to Asia Minor and Europe, but never crossing the equator.

In India they say the most beautiful woman in the world, the goddess Lakshmi, was born from a large rose, and in the East the rose was sacred to the goddess of fertility, whose priestesses wore wreaths of white roses on their heads. Confucius says there were rose gardens in ancient China and Japan, and a Chinese manuscript on roses is dated 500 BC.

The Incas in Peru, before the Spanish Conquest, grew them and called the rose-tree 'the bush of the sun'. When Christopher Columbus reached the West Indies he found roses there. But the real home of the rose in the ancient world was Persia: whole gardens were given over to it, superb rose-trees surrounded the city, the emperors themselves were skilled gardeners, and, in the luxurious Persian tradition, rich crowns were made of rose-petals stitched with raffia.

From Persia the rose was brought to Babylonia, where it was grown in the famous Hanging Gardens and became a symbol of the power of the state. There, Jewish prisoners came to know and love it. But it came very much later into Egypt and Asia Minor, and flowers that are called roses in many ancient translations should in fact be called lilies.

The rose reached Greece in the fifth century BC, and Epicurus admired it. Homer never knew it, but Sappho called it, for the first time 'the queen of flowers'. In Greek mythology it was said that Cybele created the rose because she was jealous of Aphrodite—and wished to create something more beautiful than the goddess of beauty herself. But when Aphrodite rushed to the wounded Adonis, tearing through a rose hedge and staining the flowers with her blood, the red rose was born. So the rose became the symbol of Aphrodite and of Aurora and Cupid, who accompanied her, representing love and its fleeting nature, and youth. It was also sacred to Harpocrates, the god of silence.

The Greeks were the first to use the expression that was later latinized to 'sub rosa', under the rose, to mean something secret and mysterious. This expression seems to have been used for the first time during preparations for the decisive battle of the Greeks against the Persians, which were made very secretly in a bower of roses, and although we cannot know for certain whether this story is true, we do know that the rose became a symbol of secrecy and that the term 'sub rosa' came down from ancient times into the Middle Ages, and spread all over Europe. Indeed, if a conversation were to take place in secret, a rose was hung on the ceiling, although, later on, this rose came to be made of plaster.

The Greeks considered it a flower for weddings, as well, and the women made crowns of roses, interwoven with branches of myrtle. But if it was worn on the brow or the breast, it was a sign of mourning.

From Greece the rose passed on to Rome, where it enjoyed a further period of splendour. In the early years of the Roman republic, roses were made into crowns which were worn by heroes and defenders of the state, and when the republic was in danger the wearing of roses was strictly forbidden. But later this changed, and under the Emperor Augustus roses were used in every type of decoration.

At feasts and banquets everyone, old and young, slaves, musicians and dancers, wore crowns of roses stitched with raffia; roses were twined around goblets, rose-petals dropped into the wine when toasts were drunk, and the cushions the guests sat on were filled with rose petals. Roses were used

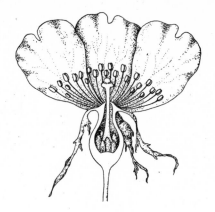

Line drawing of a wild rose flower: a simple flower, like that of the dog rose.

Section of a wild rose flower.

in the preparation of jellies, honey and wine, and rose petals were eaten crystallized.

The rose-gardens of Paestum became famous, attracting large crowds when they were in flower, and were praised by Virgil and Ovid. The Romans also looked on the rose as a symbol of love and used it to decorate their graves. In April and May, during the feast of Flora, goddess of flowers, they held celebrations in honour of the rose, and often mentioned in their wills the kinds of roses they wanted on their graves, and left bequests of money for their planting and and upkeep.

Gradually, however, the Romans' pleasure in roses became luxuriant folly. The peasants cut down their orchards and olive groves to make space for them, elaborate hothouses were built to allow them to bloom in winter, and they were brought across from Egypt by sea. Unfortunately, we know nothing about the methods by which they were transported, methods which somehow allowed them to arrive in Rome still fresh. It would seem, indeed, that the Romans' extravagance over roses was something they learned from Egypt, where Cleopatra spent vast sums in order to surround herself with roses. Suetonius says that Nero spent the equivalent of about £50,000 on roses for a single banquet; so the Romans were clearly not far behind her in lavish expense.

With the coming of Christianity this extravagance came to an end; indeed, for a short time the rose was forbidden and forgotten. But soon it returned to favour and became the loveliest decoration of the churches on religious feasts. Once again it was used as a symbol of secrecy, and in 1500 Pope Hadrian had a rose carved on all confessionals, where for some time it had been the custom to hang a real rose that had been blessed.

It seems that the prayer beads St. Dominic called 'rosaries' in 1208, which are still an object of devotion today, were first made from rose hips.

Legends grew up around the rose and many people used it symbolically. The Turks, for instance, say that the white rose originated from Mohammed's sweat and the red rose from his blood; so it is the sacred flower of the Mohammedans and until about 1750 it was the custom to wrap the babies of the Seraglio in rose-petals.

When the Roman empire in the west was overwhelmed by the barbarians, the Arabs carried on the traditions of the Persian and Babylonian gardeners and used roses extravagantly, like the ancient Romans. From about the year 1000, they managed to extract essences from roses, and to make rose-water through distillation; these scents were used to purify the mosques and other religious rooms. When North Africa and Spain were conquered the Arabs passed their love of roses on to their subject peoples.

Flowers were not considered important in the Middle Ages: people were too busy fighting and too many necessities were lacking for them to worry about the luxuries of life. But if the rose fell from favour as an ornament, it became important for its medicinal properties. Its fruit, which was rich in vitamin C, was an excellent remedy against scurvy, the most widespread of medieval diseases, and so it was grown in monasteries and spread all over Europe by the Benedictines.

It was only in France and England that the love of roses never died, in spite of wars and revolutions, and so it was in those two countries that the modern rose came into being. In France, at Fontenay-aux-roses, at Provins and in the marvellous gardens of Rouen, the Roman tradition had survived. In England a red rose, brought from France in the year 1200, was for centuries the symbol of the house of Lancaster, and a white rose symbolized the house of York. At the end of the fifteenth century, after the long and terrible Wars of the Roses, the two roses were united in the house of Tudor—and today the rose is still one of the symbols of the British royal house.

In Germany the rose had a very special symbolism. The bleeding wounds of warrior heroes were called rosebuds,

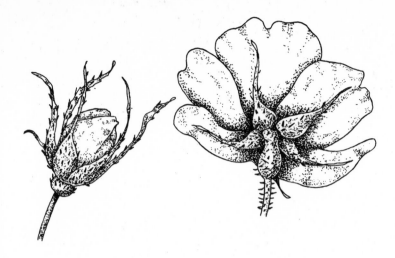

Bud with very long sepals; flower seen from below, of the Rosa macrophylla, *showing the glandular hairs which cover the calyx.*

the battlefield was known as a rose garden. Yet in the age of chivalry it was also connected with love, and love philters were distilled from roses.

After the medieval age, Europe came to a scientific period: printing was invented in Germany and botanists studied plants as they were, not as Aristotle had described them. Roses, grown according to the principles of Albert the Great and Pietro de' Crescenzi, were used in particular as hedges, and until about 1700, new flowers superseded them in many European gardens.

In eighteenth-century France, Joséphine Beauharnais, Napoleon's wife, greatly encouraged their cultivation by creating the most famous rose garden of its time at Malmaison and commissioning the famous engraver Redouté to paint pictures of the flowers. After her death the garden was left to go wild, but the roses she had made famous continued to fascinate people and many rose gardens were planted by kings and emperors during the nineteenth century.

Feasts in honour of the rose were held and its cultivation was popular everywhere; the climbing varieties on walls, artificial ruins and Gothic gateways were particular favourites. People gave presents of vases shaped as pyramids or spheres, holding very neat and regular blooms all round them.

New varieties were sold for fabulous sums during the last century, and the enthusiasm for roses has continued until our own day, when it has given rise to a specialized industry.

Today, magazines on roses, and societies like the Royal National Rose Society in England and the American Rose Society, teach people how to grow the flower and maintain its popularity. Cut roses are arranged in all kinds of ways: in bunches, in baskets, or with other flowers; from America the fashion has spread for displaying a single rose in a crystal vase. Roses are suitable for every occasion and today, as in the past, they are the very best flower for every kind of decoration both formal and informal.

A bouquet of long-stemmed roses always makes the most charming welcome for a distinguished visitor, and it is said that the then Aga Khan sent thirty thousand roses to Geneva when the League of Nations was launched. Even in the twentieth century heads of state may be welcomed by a shower of rose petals during an official visit.

Today the rose is as much of a symbol as ever, for its harmonious beauty still represents mystery, purity and love. So many associations have made this emblem of secrecy their own, like the anti-Nazi 'White Rose' group in recent years. Its regular appearance means that it is often used emblematically, for subjects that have nothing to do with botany.

And today, as in ancient times, a bunch of red roses means a declaration of love.

We now have splendid flower shops where we can find roses in the most varied colours and with the most superb scents. But in spring and summer we can also still enjoy the beautiful wild roses in the hedgerows and woods.

The principal wild roses

In hedges and on the borders of woods, in stony places, on hills and plains in many countries, we find the delightful wild roses. These are the species of roses that have not been cultivated and have remained in their natural state. There are thought to be between one hundred and fifty and two hundred species, but it is difficult to be certain. Over the centuries, wild roses have cross-bred through pollination by insects, producing sub-species that should really be called hybrids. Many of these are still known as species, because it is impossible to be quite sure whether they are or not.

Species of wild roses come in many forms, from very small, twiggy bushes to huge shrubs with long, arching canes and strong, hooked thorns. Often they have leaves consisting of seven leaflets instead of the five usually found in cultivated roses. All species flower only once a year, the

Buds and flower of the Rosa involucrata: *note the completely bare stalk and calyx.*

blooms of most coming in either June or July, though there are some which flower in May. True species only have simple, single flowers with five petals, and those so-called species with double flowers are almost certainly sub-species hybrids. Generally the flowers come in great profusion, either singly or in clusters all along the branches. The most common colours are white or pink, but there are yellow and bright red ones as well.

The fruit of the rose is called the hip or hep, and most wild roses have very attractive hips in late summer and autumn when the flowers are over. These can be almost globular, oval, or in some cases shaped like flagons and as much as two inches long. As they may be bright red, yellow or orange they make a gay display, and a few of the roses actually have more decorative hips than flowers.

As there are so many of them, it is only possible to mention here a few of the species by name. One of the commonest is *Rosa canina*, the dog rose, so called because the Romans believed that it had properties that would cure rabies. It grows in hedgerows and open woodland at heights of up to 3,000 feet above sea level, flowering in May and June according to the latitude. There are several forms with either deep pink, blush pink or white petals. Another common rose of central Europe is *R. arvensis*. It has slender reddish-mauve branches and white flowers in June and July. In mountain scrubland grows *R. cinnamomea*, a tall bush with large pink flowers in clusters. *R. pendulina* (synonymous with *R. alpina*) grows even higher up and flowers later, in July and August. It has purplish-pink flowers and few thorns. *R. spinosissima* in its many forms will grow in the poorest soils and will thrive on sand dunes. The flowers are generally yellow or white.

The flowers of *R. moschata* are white and have a strong musk fragrance; coming originally from the east, it has become naturalized on the shores of the Mediterranean. *R. rubiganosa*, parent of a range of garden shrubs known as Penzance Roses after Lord Penzance who introduced them,

has resinous glands in its leaves that give out a smell like that of russet apples.

In Italy, *R. sempervirens*, which also originated, like so many of them, in the east, is another that has naturalized itself. It has white flowers and a strong scent, and it flowers in May and June. Across the Atlantic, one of the best-known American species, *R. virginiana*, has leaves that turn to wonderful flame colours in the autumn.

These are just a very few of the species of wild roses found in Europe, Asia and America. Surprisingly, it would seem that only a very few of them have played an important part in the development of cultivated roses, but a great many of them make striking garden shrubs in their natural, unadulterated form. Today, thanks to the work of some nurserymen, they are available for the domestic garden.

The development of the garden rose

Through selection and hybridization a great many types of rose have been developed from a small number of species. These vary enormously in form, in colour and in their behaviour. Roses from the east played a big part in the story of the garden rose, but many of these were certainly hybrids already, themselves developed over many centuries.

It is generally considered that three species or sub-species, *R. gallica*, *R. damescena* and *R. alba*, the first of the three being the oldest, are the roses from which most garden forms are descended. Until comparatively recently it was also believed that *R. centifolia* was also one of the very old ones; in fact that it was the 'hundred leaves rose' described by the Greeks and the Romans, but it is now known to have been developed in Holland in the eighteenth century. The older rose has obviously been lost some time in the more distant past. The first Moss Rose *(R. centifolia muscosa)* was a sport or mutation from *R. centifolia* which also occurred

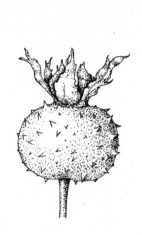

Left: Rose hip, shaped like an ampoule. Right: Spurious fruit: hip of the dog rose.

Left: Rose hip, globular, flattened top and bottom, with thorns. Right: Rose hip, globular and spiral.

in the Netherlands, from which both spread to the rest of the world.

R. gallica may have been brought from Asia to Europe by the Romans. It spread to Northern France and was so widely grown round the town of Provins for its medicinal properties that it became known as the Provins Rose. It was cultivated all through the Middle Ages as a medicinal plant and was taken to England by the Duke of Lancaster, where its red flower became part of the coat of arms of the Kings of England. The early settlers probably took it to America.

The Damask Rose *(R. damascena)*, noted for its sweet perfume, was brought by the Greeks to Marseilles, Carthage and Paestum, and was much prized by the Romans. It was at Paestum in Italy that one of its hybrids was seen to be blooming in the autumn as well as the summer, so the Romans called it *R. bifera*, and the French, a good deal later, 'rose des quatre saisons'. Huge quantities were destroyed by the eruption of Vesuvius that overwhelmed Pompeii, and with the decline of the Roman Empire its widespread planting dwindled. However, the Arabs continued to cultivate it and obtained rose water from it, and eventually it reappeared in the west, possibly brought in from the Middle East by the Crusaders.

A real revolution in garden roses took place at the end of the eighteenth century with the arrival from the Far East of the China Roses, and with the discovery that plants could be crossed artificially. Up until then only one rose, *R. damascena bifera* (mentioned above), was known to flower more than once, but the China Roses bloomed regularly a second time and in much greater profusion, for the Damask Rose was rather half-hearted in its second blooming. So the China Roses were used to achieve what had only been dreamed of before: garden roses that flowered most of the summer.

Prominent in the history of roses is the Bourbon Rose, with its large, many-petalled flowers, which came from the Ile de Bourbon (now Réunion) in the Indian Ocean. This

was the result of a chance natural cross between a China Rose and a Damask, but its good qualities were soon recognized and it became very popular. Crossed once more with hybrids of the China Roses, it created the family of Hybrid Perpetuals, most of which repeated well and were considered to be perpetual flowering in contrast to what had gone before. They spread with great rapidity all over the world, but few of them have survived for they were, after a while, crossed with another arrival from the east, the not-too-hardy Tea Rose. The result was the even longer and more profusely blooming Hybrid Teas such as we know today and the classic, high-centred type of bloom that we so much admire.

Up to the beginning of this century, almost all garden roses were in shades of red, pink, maroon, mauve, purple or white, with a few very insipid pale yellows amongst the Teas. Then, in 1885, a French nurseryman named Pernet Ducher began a series of experimental crosses with a Persian bright yellow species, *R. foetida* and its red and yellow sport, *R. foetida bicolor*. A sport is a chance shoot appearing on a rose bush which produces flowers of a different colour and sometimes of a different form from those of the rest of the bush; this is caused by the characteristics of one of the ancestors of that particular rose showing themselves again. *R. foetida* was a single rose and did not prove to be an easy one to cross with the Hybrid Perpetuals of the time. Again and again nothing resulted, but Pernet Ducher persisted and, fifteen years later, in 1900, he had his reward. He produced Soleil d'Or, a rich orange-yellow rose with double flowers like a Hybrid Perpetual. From this he went on again until, in 1920, he unveiled his masterpiece, Souvenir de Claudius Pernet, a true yellow rose, named after his son who had been killed in the war.

These early yellow roses, by Pernet Ducher and others that followed him, had little resistance to diseases and frost, and tended to be short-lived, but from them are descended all the yellow, orange and flame roses that we know today.

9

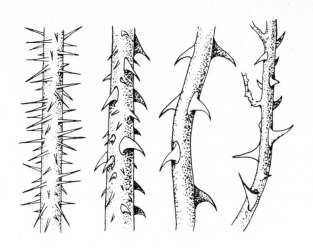

Unfortunately a lot of them have also inherited from *R. foetida* a strong tendency towards black spot.

Many of the older species of roses—often now known collectively as shrub roses—are still grown in gardens and are becoming increasingly popular. A great many of them continue to be known by their Latin names, but modern roses have names chosen by their raisers. Some of them are pretty odd, and they certainly do not help to trace the ancestry of a particular rose as many of the old names did.

Climbing and rambling roses have ancestors coming mostly from the east like *R. gigantica*, *R. moschata* (the true Musk Rose), *R. multiflora* and *R. wichuraiana*. These and rambling roses are useful, if given some support, to cover fences, pillars, walls and pergolas, and are used in America in particular as anti-dazzle and crash barriers on the big highways. The flowers of climbing roses are large and double, like those of Hybrid Teas, or they can be semi-double or single. Sometimes they grow in clusters—the flowers of ramblers always do, and they flower once only, whereas some climbers repeat or are more or less perpetual. Some climbers, like Dortmund, Golden Showers and Aloha, are not very tall and can be grown as large, spreading shrubs.

A chance cross with Japanese *multiflora* roses produced dwarf varieties known as Polyantha Pompons. All of them were very small (though not as small as the real miniatures, the early history of which is not known) and had large numbers of tiny flowers in clusters. Most of them were scentless, but they were popular as pot plants. In due course these Polyanthas were crossed with Hybrid Teas by the Danish rose grower Svend Poulsen, and the result was the much larger Hybrid Polyantha roses, which later became known as Floribundas.

Today these are some of the most popular roses in our gardens. Their flowers grow in clusters or trusses, sometimes of tremendous size, with twenty or thirty blooms. These blooms can be double, semi-double or single and, because of their comparatively short petals, they open much more freely than Hybrid Teas in wet weather. Individually, the flowers may not have the same fine form (though this is now being bred into them) but for mass bedding display they are unbeatable. The best of them repeat very quickly, they are hardy, and they need little looking after. This serves in part to explain their undoubted popularity.

The largest and the smallest rose

Roses vary enormously in size, but if one wants to determine the largest and the smallest, some definition of large and small is needed.

If by large we mean the greatest number of petals, probably the Hybrid Tea, Baccara, wins, with up to eighty-two, though the resulting flowers are by no means the largest in overall size. Almost any Hybrid Tea can throw a gigantic bloom occasionally, but varieties like Peace, and the rather rare Big Ben, will have them constantly. Among Floribundas, Ascot has only semi-double flowers, but they are about 4 inches across.

There is no doubt at all about the rose with the fewest petals. *R. sericea pteracantha* has only four and is the only rose with less than five. Some of the smallest rose flowers are no more than half an inch in diameter. Shrubs like Ballerina have these, and the miniature, Sweet Fairy, must have both the smallest bush and the smallest flowers. It grows not much over six inches high and its blooms are about half an inch across.

Some climbers, descendants of roses from China and the Himalayas (*R. moschata* and *R. brunonii*), can reach forty or fifty feet when scrambling up and through a tall tree, and amongst shrubs Frühlingsgold will top eight feet and spread out as far all round. Queen Elizabeth is just about the tallest Floribunda (or Grandiflora according to where you live), and Uncle Walter the tallest Hybrid Tea.

10

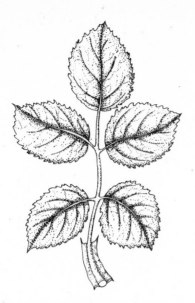

Schematic drawing of a spray of rose leaves, consisting of five small oval serrated leaves: the stalk has no thorns.

Leaf of Rosa indica, *var.* ruga: *a hybrid between* Rosa chinensis *and* Rosa arvensis. *The stalk is prickly: as in other roses, there may be an even number of leaves because one of those in the end pair is missing.*

It should be stressed, however, that size will vary quite considerably in the same varieties according to climate, soil, and the general conditions in which they are grown.

The rose in the garden

From early summer to late autumn the rose is the finest ornament in any garden, and Hybrid Teas and Floribundas are particularly suitable for planting in beds where you want a mass of colour over a very long period, without the bother of planting out each year, as you have to do with annual bedding plants. On average, rose bushes should be planted about eighteen inches apart, although with very vigorous varieties like Peace, and with those that spread out a long way, like the Floribunda Sarabande, this should be increased to about two feet. It is usually considered best to keep to one variety in each bed, but in a big border this can be varied by planting several varieties in groups of five or six, not forgetting to have colours that blend well next to each other. A few standard or tree-roses can give an interesting variation of height in the centre of an isolated bed.

The taller Hybrid Teas and Floribundas, and of course the bigger shrub roses, are very useful for decorative, flowering hedges and screens. The planting distance between them should be about half the eventual spread of the rose.

Climbing roses make a good cover for walls of houses and for walls surrounding a garden. There are several that will bloom well, even on a north wall. They will need the support of wires and should be trained as near to the horizontal as possible, fanning the canes out in both directions along the wall. In this way, new shoots will be encouraged to come lower down, and the flowers will not all be at the top.

Ramblers tend to mildew badly on a wall as they do not have sufficient air circulation, but they, together with the climbers, can be used for pillars, trellises and pergolas.

If a rose is being trained on a pillar, the canes should be wound round it in a spiral, which again will have the effect of making it bloom low down as well as at the top.

If you have the space, it is quite useful to have a special bed of roses for cutting for the house, but pick varieties that are known to last well and that have good, strong flower stalks.

Famous rose gardens

Many nurseries have special display gardens where you can see the varieties they sell growing as they will in your garden. Those in the nursery beds will be young and not fully developed plants, from which it is difficult to judge final performance. There are also a number of famous rose gardens all over the world where the public can go and see what they would like to have for themselves. It is much safer to choose your roses in this way.

There are some amateur rose breeders, but most of the hybridizing is done by the nursery trade. The constant search for something new takes infinite patience—the quest for a blue rose for instance—and if a breeder comes up with something that he thinks is worth while, he will send it for trial or enter it in one or more of the competitions for new roses that are held in the world's most famous rose centres.

Each cross between two roses produces a number of seeds and there may be thousands of crosses carried out each season between different roses in one nursery alone. The chances of producing a winner are reckoned to be something of the order of 20,000 to 1. At the Meilland gardens in Antibes, for instance, forty-five thousand seedlings are grown each year and, through selection, these may be reduced to three or four varieties which are worth putting on the market. All this, of course, is because of the mixed ancestry of the rose which makes certain results quite impossible.

Every year about two hundred new roses are produced

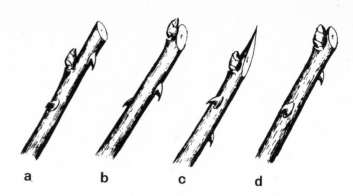

all over the world, and put on the market. But before this most of them will undergo at least three years of trial at a rose centre where competitions are held. Some gardens award certificates and some give prizes and cups and medals for the best roses, which are then protected and patented.

One of the most famous rose gardens is that of the Jackson and Perkins company at Newark, New Jersey. In Europe there is a famous rose garden at Geneva and another in the Bagatelle park in Paris. Further south, in Lyons, is another garden where the competition is limited to French raised varieties and there is also the famous Roseraie de l'Hay, which includes a rose museum.

The most beautiful rose garden in the world is said to be that of the Oeste Park in Madrid, which dates from 1954. In England there is the well-known Queen Mary's Rose Garden in Regent's Park in London, and the Royal National Rose Society's garden at St Albans, where rose trials are held.

In Italy, a competition is held in the rose garden in Rome, planted in 1928 on the ruins of the Domus Aurea and enlarged in 1948. Yet another famous garden is in Turin; this is part of the Valentino Gardens and was planted in 1961 to celebrate the centenary of the unification of the Kingdom of Italy.

How to grow roses

The rose has one very important quality. Through its wide natural distribution over the centuries, it is very adaptable and can be grown in almost every type of garden. Probably a good heavy loam is best for it. The myth that roses must have clay is—a myth. They will do perfectly well even on light, sandy soil, though they will need a little extra feeding.

Preparation of the ground must be thorough. In a bed that is intended for roses, a trench about eighteen inches wide should be dug at one end, and the soil deposited at the other end. Make certain the soil at the bottom of the trench is well broken up, and incorporate some well-rotted manure or compost into it. Fill in the trench, making another one alongside it as you do so, so working right across the bed and filling in the last trench with the soil you took out of the first one. This should be done as early in the autumn as possible so that the ground has time to settle again before planting begins.

Planting may be done immediately after leaf fall, when the bushes are dormant. This is likely to be from mid-November onwards, which is really the best time. However, it can be carried on right through the winter and up to March, provided you choose a time when there is no likelihood of frost and when the ground is not waterlogged.

If the roses arrive from the nursery with their roots dry they should be soaked for about an hour before planting. For the actual planting, dig a hole sufficiently wide for the roots to be well spread out in it and put the rose in the hole so that the union between the bud and the stock is just below soil level—generally the stock is indicated by a swelling just above the roots, from which the canes are growing. Fill up the hole with soil mixed with a little damp peat and a handful of rose fertilizer. Tread in firmly but not too hard.

In February or March, established rose beds should be dressed with bonemeal or the fertilizer you used in planting, gently hoeing it in. Depending on the quality of your soil, further dressings should be given at two or three regular intervals until the middle of July. Any fertilizer given after that will only encourage late growth which is likely to be damaged by frost in the coming winter, as it will not have had a chance to ripen properly. Always hoe the fertilizer in, but only do this lightly or the delicate feeding roots of the rose, which are comparatively near the surface, will be damaged.

Rose beds should either be hoed frequently throughout the season to control weeds or else mulched with damp peat;

 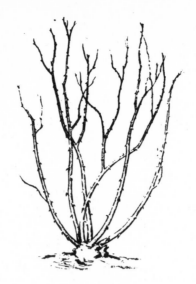 

this is better, though more expensive, as it conserves moisture as well. The mulch will smother the weeds and help to maintain an even soil temperature. Well-rotted compost also makes a good mulch if you can make enough of it.

Pests and diseases

Probably the most serious pest that the average rose grower will have to contend with is the aphis or greenfly, which sucks sap from young growth. Caterpillars can be another menace, but if there are not too many of them—and if you do not have too many roses—they can be picked off by hand and destroyed. Pesticides are available to control most insect pests.

Sudden changes of temperature or dryness at the roots may bring on an attack of mildew. As soon as it is noticed it should be controlled by spraying with a proprietary fungicide. Continue at fortnightly intervals as long as the attack lasts. More serious are black spot and rust, which may result in the loss of leaves and which can even kill a plant in time. Dark, black spots on the leaves indicate the former and orange pustules under the leaves the latter. They occur usually in mid- to late summer and can again be controlled by spraying. If rust is really bad, however, the bushes should be dug up and burned.

Pruning

Pruning is necessary to encourage strong new growth, which in turn results in better and bigger blooms. It also keeps the bush in a good shape. Pruning can be done at almost any time during the winter provided that there is no frost about, but most people do it in February or March in temperate climates. In cold areas it is likely to be later, but the important thing is to complete it before vigorous new growth really starts in the spring. In November, when roses for pot culture are lifted and potted, shorten the shoots to one, two or three 'eyes' from the base, according to size.

Hybrid Teas: Remove all weak and spindly growth and shorten the remainder to three to five buds, cutting to an outward-facing eye except with varieties that sprawl. Newly-planted bushes should be cut to two or three buds, which encourages the development of roots before the top growth.

Floribundas: Prune rather more lightly than for Hybrid Teas, cutting to the first or second bud below an old flower truss on strong growth and more severely on the weaker canes. Again cut out all weak and spindly wood and thin out the centre of the bush if it is growing very thickly, to let in air.

Ramblers: After they have flowered in the summer, and if there are plenty of new canes coming from the base, cut out all the old ones, right to the ground. Otherwise cut back the old canes by about one third. Never do more than tip back the canes of newly planted ramblers or climbers, particularly if they are climbing sports.

Climbers: These will generally do very well with no pruning at all, but they can have their side shoots cut back by about one third in order to thin them out if they are growing very thickly.

Standards or Tree Roses: Prune as for a Hybrid Tea or Floribunda (according to which variety of standard it is), but rather more severely as growth will usually be weaker. Remove any side growths that appear on the stem.

Weeping Standards: Prune as for ramblers.

Rose Species: No regular pruning required, except for the removal of old, dead wood from time to time.

Shrub or Old Fashioned Roses: For most of them, follow the advice given for species, but there are exceptions so it would be best to ask your nurseryman for advice.

Summer Pruning or Dead-heading: To encourage a second crop of flowers it helps if the old blooms are removed. But do not just pull off the old flowers. Cut back to the first healthy-looking bud below them.

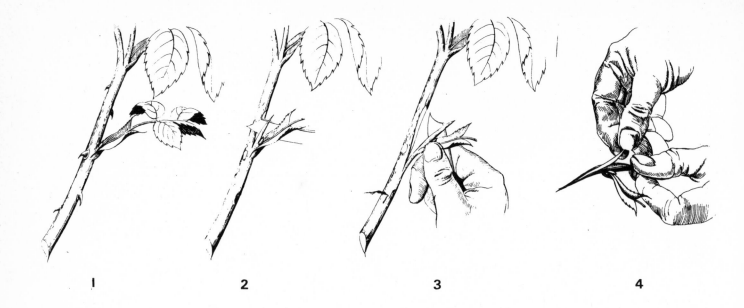

1   2   3   4

Autumn Pruning: This is not true pruning, but the reduction of all strong growth on tall-growing roses by about one third in October and November. This prevents them being rocked about in the winter winds. If they do rock, soil at the base of the plant becomes compacted into a small funnel, in which water can gather and freeze, which could kill the rose.

Removal of Suckers: Suckers are growths coming from the wild rose which forms the stock, below the point where the bud was inserted. They are not always easy to recognise, but often have seven leaves and the leaves are lighter in colour. If you suspect a sucker, scrape away a little of the soil and try to trace it back to its source. This is the only way to be sure, until you know what you are looking for. Pull it away. Cutting it will only encourage new growth, for sucker buds will be left behind. So will cutting a sucker at soil level. Replace the soil and press it in.

Winter Protection: In countries that have very cold winters, for instance in parts of the United States, it is necessary to give your rose bushes some winter protection. This may consist in heaping earth over the base of the bush and wrapping the heads of tree roses in straw or dried bracken, tied in firmly so that it does not blow away. In Britain, roses can be protected by drawing up soil round the base to a height of six inches, or by putting dry litter among the shoots.

The rose in the life of man

In ancient times and in the Middle Ages love philters were made from roses; but quite apart from this magical use, roses were used as excellent deodorants, in times when washing was unfashionable. Even today, small sachets of dried rose petals are sometimes still put in the linen cupboard.

In ancient Rome, roses were used in the preparation of jellies, honey, wine and desserts, and today the fruit of the dog rose is used to make preserves and jam. In the east, their petals are used in the making of sweets and to flavour liqueurs and ice-creams.

The important medicinal qualities of roses were already known in Roman times, and in the Middle Ages all apothecaries used them because their fruit was rich in what we now know as vitamin C.

Today rose water has a pharmaceutical use in the cure of eye diseases; the petals of *Rosa centifolia* are used in laxatives for children, and those of *Rosa gallica* provide astringent liquids and are used in rose hip syrup.

Rose water and essences made from roses are most useful of all in the perfume industry, which came to us from the east—from Arabia and Persia in particular. Rose water is extracted from *Rosa moschata*, *Rosa damascena* and others, by rapid distillation with steam or a solvent, and this is used to purify and improve the skin; distilled again, it becomes an essence used in perfumes.

The perfume industry is important in Nice and Cannes, and even more so in Eastern Europe and the near east—in Bulgaria and Turkey mainly; but recently the production of artificial essences has hit it hard.

The rose in this century is important as a decoration, and thousands of people, including rose experts, are employed in producing cut flowers, potted bushes and garden plants. The Dutch, who produce flowers that are entirely uniform and very predictable in their behaviour and quality, are supremely successful in the cultivation of roses.

In the realm of art the impact of the rose is found in poetry, painting, sculpture, jewellery and all forms of decoration. Writers, poets and playwrights have used it symbolically in their work in a variety of ways.

Recommended roses listed by colour

Most, though not quite all, of these roses are described in detail in the colour pages of this book. All should give a good display in the average garden, but it should be remem-

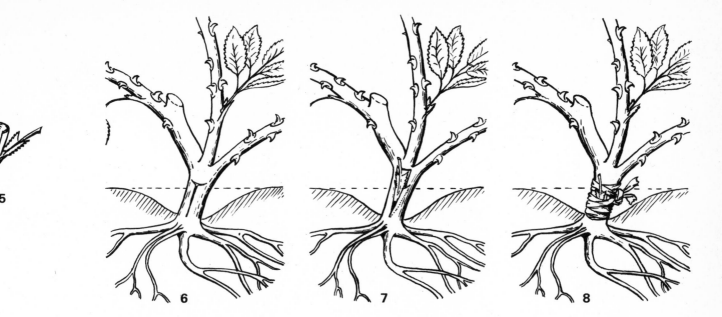

5

6 7 8

bered that not all soils and not all climates suit all roses equally well. Some will always do better than others, according to conditions. The only way to be sure that a rose will give you of its best is to ask advice locally from someone who knows, or to try growing the roses yourself. Nine times out of ten you will be lucky. The roses below are grouped by colour, as an aid when planning a colour scheme.

WHITE
Handel Climber, white flushed pink.
Iceberg Floribunda, tall.
Ice White Floribunda, medium height.
Pascali Hybrid Tea.

YELLOW
Allgold Floribunda, low-growing, unfading.
Arthur Bell Floribunda, tall, fades to cream.
Buccaneer Hybrid Tea or Grandiflora, tall-growing.
Casino Climber, perpetual, scented.
China Town Floribunda or shrub, very tall.
Circus Floribunda, yellow, orange and pink tints.
Elegance Climber, once-flowering, very vigorous.
Gold Crown Hybrid Tea, tall.
Golden Showers Short climber or shrub, perpetual.
Grandpa Dickson (Irish Gold) Hybrid Tea, pale yellow.
King's Ransom Hybrid Tea.
Peace Hybrid Tea, very large, pale yellow tinted pink.
Sutter's Gold Hybrid Tea, tall, yellow, flushed and splashed red. Good for bedding.
Yellow Cushion Floribunda, fragrant.

BRIGHT RED
Alec's Red Hybrid Tea.
Champs Elysées Hybrid Tea.
City of Belfast Floribunda.
Danse du Feu (Spectacular) Climber.
Dortmund Climber, red with white eye, single.
Ernest H. Morse Hybrid Tea, very free bloomer.
Evelyn Fison (Irish Wonder) Floribunda, unfading and rainproof. A strong plant that gives a fine show.

Fragrant Cloud Hybrid Tea, geranium red.
Lilli Marlene Floribunda.
Marlene Floribunda, short.
Red Planet Hybrid Tea, exhibition quality.
Sarabande Floribunda, spreading.
Summer Holiday Hybrid Tea. A less tall and healthier Super Star (Tropicana).
Super Star (Tropicana) Hybrid Tea. Still worth growing in an area where it does not get mildew.

DARK RED
Chrysler Imperial Hybrid Tea.
Europeana Floribunda, low and spreading.
Josephine Bruce Hybrid Tea, low and spreading.
Mister Lincoln Hybrid Tea, tall.
Parade Climber.
Paprika Floribunda.

PINK
Albertine Rambler/climber, very vigorous.
Aloha Short climber or shrub.
Anna Louisa Floribunda.
Bantry Bay Climber.
Border Coral Floribunda.
Dearest Floribunda, not rain-proof, but a charmer.
Elizabeth of Glamis (Irish Beauty) Floribunda, salmon-pink. Perfectly symmetrical buds.
First Love Hybrid Tea, deep pink.
Mischief Hybrid Tea, salmon-pink.
Mullard Jubilee Hybrid Tea, deep pink.
Paddy McGredy Floribunda-Hybrid Tea Type, low growing with an abundance of blooms.
Perfecta Hybrid Tea, pink and cream.
Pink Favourite Hybrid Tea, very healthy.
Pink Parfait Floribunda-Hybrid Tea Type or Grandiflora, tall. Good for flower arrangement.
Pink Perpetue Climber.
Prima Ballerina Hybrid Tea, satin-pink, strong fragrance.
Queen Elizabeth Floribunda-Hybrid Tea Type or Grandi-

flora. Very tall and therefore good for backgrounds.

Royal Highness Hybrid Tea, palest blush-pink.

Stella Hybrid Tea or Grandiflora. Pink and cream, rainproof. Good for bedding.

Violet Carson Floribunda-Hybrid Tea Type, peach-yellow reverse. Lasts well as cut flowers.

Wendy Cussons Hybrid Tea, cerise-pink.

RED AND YELLOW

Masquerade Floribunda.

My Choice Hybrid Tea, pale pink and primrose.

Gail Borden Hybrid Tea, apricot and primrose.

Paintbox Floribunda, low-growing.

Piccadilly Hybrid Tea.

PINK AND WHITE

Molly McGredy Floribunda.

Rose Gaujard Hybrid Tea.

ORANGE

Beauté Hybrid Tea.

Bettina Hybrid Tea.

Doreen Hybrid Tea, low-growing.

Mojave Hybrid Tea, sunset colours, tall.

Orangeade Floribunda, vermilion-orange.

Orange Sensation Floribunda, vermilion-orange.

Zambra Floribunda, orange, yellow reverse, low-growing.

PEACH

Apricot Nectar Floribunda.

Chicago Peace Hybrid Tea, strong grower, tall.

CREAM

Chanelle Floribunda, flushed pink.

Ivory Fashion Floribunda.

MAUVE

Blue Moon Hybrid Tea.

In the pages that follow, over one hundred roses are described. Most can be obtained from your local nursery, but a few are not easy to get and a search will have to be made for them in the rose-growers' catalogues. In the descriptions the name of the rose is given first, together with alternative names it may have in different countries. Next comes the classification, e.g., Hybrid Tea, the name of the breeder who raised it, and the date of introduction. Finally, before the actual description, comes the parentage of the rose. Charlotte Armstrong X Floradora means that two roses bearing these names were crossed to produce the rose described in the caption. Golden Rapture X (Max Krause X Captain Thomas) means that the last two roses were crossed to produce a rose that was never named or put on the market. It had, however, good qualities, and was crossed in turn with Golden Rapture, the result being, in this particular case, Buccaneer. It is sometimes useful to know the parentage of your roses. For instance, the vigorous offspring of Peace should not be pruned too hard, generally speaking, and this applies to Peace itself. If in doubt about the extent of pruning, ask your nurseryman.

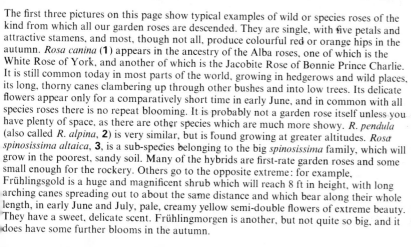

R. centifolia muscosa (**4**) is the original form of the Moss Rose, which was enormously popular in Victorian times. Its buds and flower stalks are covered in numerous little pointed glands which are sticky and scented and resemble moss if you do not look too closely. R. centifolia muscosa was a sport from one of the older centifolia roses and is pink, but there are also white, deep red and pink and white striped forms.

The first three pictures on this page show typical examples of wild or species roses of the kind from which all our garden roses are descended. They are single, with five petals and attractive stamens, and most, though not all, produce colourful red or orange hips in the autumn. Rosa canina (**1**) appears in the ancestry of the Alba roses, one of which is the White Rose of York, and another of which is the Jacobite Rose of Bonnie Prince Charlie. It is still common today in most parts of the world, growing in hedgerows and wild places, its long, thorny canes clambering up through other bushes and into low trees. Its delicate flowers appear only for a comparatively short time in early June, and in common with all species roses there is no repeat blooming. It is probably not a garden rose itself unless you have plenty of space, as there are other species which are much more showy. R. pendula (also called R. alpina, **2**) is very similar, but is found growing at greater altitudes. Rosa spinosissima altaica, **3**, is a sub-species belonging to the big spinosissima family, which will grow in the poorest, sandy soil. Many of the hybrids are first-rate garden roses and some small enough for the rockery. Others go to the opposite extreme: for example, Frühlingsgold is a huge and magnificent shrub which will reach 8 ft in height, with long arching canes spreading out to about the same distance and which bear along their whole length, in early June and July, pale, creamy yellow semi-double flowers of extreme beauty. They have a sweet, delicate scent. Frühlingmorgen is another, but not quite so big, and it does have some further blooms in the autumn.

5 Pascali Hybrid Tea. Lens, 1963. Queen Elizabeth × White Butterfly. The only white Hybrid Tea to stand rain well and be reasonably free from disease. It has medium-sized, high-centred flowers, which sometimes have a touch of cream in their colouring. Strong and upright to 3 ft. Glossy, dark green leaves. Good for cutting.

8

9

10

6 Queen Elizabeth Floribunda (UK) or Grandiflora (USA). Lammerts, 1954. Charlotte Armstrong × Floradora. One of the tallest of roses and not really suitable for bedding, as it can grow up to 9 ft or so, though fairly hard pruning can keep it below this. The foliage is dark and handsome, semi-glossy and generally healthy. The flowers are of a soft, light pink. Sometimes they come in medium-sized clusters and sometimes singly, but always on long stalks, which makes them suitable for cutting. Only slight fragrance. For the back of the border or for a hedge.

7 Iceberg Floribunda. Kordes, 1958. Robin Hood × Virgo. (Also known as Schneewittchen and Fée des Neiges). The white blooms, shaped like those of a camellia, are carried all over the bush and not just at the top as in so many Floribundas. They come in medium-sized trusses on the rather slender branches, and the bush is rarely out of flower. It may reach 6 ft unless pruned. Some mildew and some black spot are possible, but rarely bad. One of the very best roses, which will stand up to prolonged rain very well.

8 Percy Thrower Hybrid Tea. Lens, 1964. La Jolla × Karl Herbst. Large, fragrant, rose-pink, well-formed double flowers on a vigorously growing bush that is, however, inclined to sprawl. This means that in wet weather the blooms tend to droop, and pruning the canes to an inward-facing eye is needed to keep the plant more compact. The foliage is dark green and glossy.

9 Royal Highness Hybrid Tea. Swim and Weeks, 1962. Virgo × Peace. Also known as Königliche Hoheit. A very upright grower which will reach 5 ft and not spread out very much. It is a profuse bloomer, with beautifully shaped, high-centred flowers of such a soft light pink that they give the impression of being white from a distance. They are not very good in wet weather, but when cut hold their perfect form for a very long time. For this reason it is a favourite rose with exhibitors on both sides of the Atlantic. Very dark green, leathery foliage, which is reasonably healthy.

10 Invitation Hybrid Tea. Swim and Weeks, 1961. Charlotte Armstrong × Signora. Long, pointed buds develop into 4½ in, double, high-centred flowers of a rich salmon-pink, merging into yellow at the petal bases. A compact and bushy grower, free blooming, and with good, glossy foliage. Strongly scented.

11 Mischief Hybrid Tea. McGredy, 1961. Peace ×
Spartan. This is one of the best bedding roses. It is healthy,
vigorous but not too tall, and almost continually in flower.
The blooms can be up to 4 ins across, but when they come in
clusters, as they tend to do especially in the autumn, they are
likely to be rather smaller. However, they are almost always
well-shaped with a good high centre, and at their best and
biggest can be used for showing. They are fragrant and of a
strong, salmon-pink, and grow on a strong, upright bush of
about 2 ft 6 ins or a little more. The light green foliage is
generally healthy. This rose is the winner of a number of top
national awards, and fully deserving of them.

12 Jenny Fair Hybrid Tea. De Ruiter, 1967. Tropicana ×
unknown. Rather globular pink flowers which are well
scented. They grow on a rather slender and upright bush and
are well set off by the dark foliage, which may need watching
for mildew. Free blooming, but not really bushy enough to
make it the best of bedding roses.

13 Dr. Albert Schweitzer Hybrid Tea. Delbert-Chabert,
1961. Chic Parisien × Michèle Meilland. Large, 5–6 in
flowers of 30 to 35 petals, and of a light cerise-pink with a
paler reverse. They are well formed on opening but can
become rather loose after a short time. A very vigorous,
upright bush with dark, glossy foliage, which is very good for
bedding and gives an especially impressive autumn display,
though it may be affected by both mildew and black spot. The
flowers are fragrant.

14

15

14 City of Leeds Floribunda. McGredy, 1966. Evelyn Fison × (Spartan × Red Favourite). This is a comparatively new rose and as such it is unwise to be too dogmatic about its qualities. It can take a number of years for a rose to settle down and show its true form (see Super Star), but certainly City of Leeds does look like a winner and it has a first-rate floribunda, Evelyn Fison (Irish Wonder in the USA) as one of its parents. The rich salmon flowers are carried on good-sized trusses, and come very freely with a quick repeat, but they can spot after prolonged rain. The plant is of upright growth with dark green foliage, which is generally quite healthy. Little or no scent.

15 Love Token Floribunda. Gregory, 1964. Parentage not known, which means it is probably a chance seedling, for which the bees were responsible. A good rose for all weathers as it is practically rain-proof. The trusses of peach-pink flowers are well-spaced; the flowers themselves are of medium size and double, though they have little scent. Growth is vigorous and spreading and the leaves large, dark and glossy. When young they have an attractive purplish tinge. Not particularly prone to any of the usual rose diseases.

16 Tip Top Floribunda. Tantau, 1963. Parentage not known, but this particular German breeder quite often does not give particulars of his breeding lines. This rose should not be confused with the miniature rose known as Tip-Top, and in fact, registration of its name was rejected because it was found that the miniature was still in commerce. However, despite all this, it is a good rose with well-formed, double, salmon-pink, scented blooms which grow in very large clusters and very freely. The growth is strong and bushy, on the low side, which makes it very suitable for small beds, though it can make a spectacular display in a large one. Medium-green leaves.

17 **Vilia** Floribunda. Robinson, 1960. Parentage unknown.
Large clusters of single, coral-pink flowers, very freely borne.
They are scented, though not strongly, and come on a
moderately vigorous bush with dark green, glossy foliage. It is
a good bloomer in the autumn.

18 **Super Star** (Tropicana in the USA). Hybrid Tea.
Tantau, 1960. (Seedling × Peace) × (Seedling × Alpine
Glow). This is a rose that took the gardening world by storm,
for its light vermilion blooms were of a colour never before
seen in roses and have, in addition, an almost luminous
quality which makes them stand out against all others. A
number of roses have been bred from it since then, and have
almost captured its unique colouring, but not quite, and
certainly none of them can equal Super Star's four Gold
Medals and numerous other awards. The flowers may come
singly (in which case they will be large, up to 5 ins at their
best and of the high-pointed form that makes them good for
showing) or in clusters, particularly in the autumn. They last
for a long time in water and have a sweet scent. They are
produced very freely on an extremely vigorous bush, which is
likely to grow to about 3 ft 6 ins or 4 ft, with dark, glossy,
leathery foliage. All this on the credit side, but Super Star is
not a rose that has worn well, at least in some areas. It
appeared for a number of years to be extremely healthy –
with its other qualities, to be nearly perfect, in fact – but
then, for no apparent reason, it started to get mildew badly,
and this is a continuing trait; however it does not occur
everywhere it is grown, so that the rose is worth taking a
chance with. There is a climbing version, or sport, on the
market as well.

17

18

20

21

19 Dearest Floribunda. Dickson, 1960. (Seedling × Spartan). Getting the worst over first, this rose does not like rain, which is unusual in a Floribunda – though surprisingly it does well in the autumn, when the air tends to be damp. But apart from this one fault, it has everything to recommend it and has long been a favourite. The clusters of very large and very double flowers, freely borne, are of the most enchanting rosy salmon shade, and scented. They grow on a strong, upright bush to about 2 ft 6 ins, on which the foliage is dark and glossy and not particularly prone to disease. During a long hot summer you will get an almost non-stop display, and it will carry on flowering into the late months of the year, even until the first frost of winter.

20 Tombola Floribunda. De Ruiter, 1967. Amor × (Ena Harkness × Peace). The truss has large, well-shaped flowers in the half-open stage but they do not keep their good form when open. However, this does not matter too much as the overall effect of the truss is a fine blend of salmon-orange with a touch of light carmine and gold at the bases of the petals of each flower. The bush is strong-growing, rather upright, and the leaves are a good, glossy green. Not, unfortunately, very quick to repeat.

21 Elizabeth of Glamis (Irish Beauty) Floribunda. McGredy, 1964. Spartan × Highlight. Her Royal Highness, the Queen Mother, gave her permission for this rose to be named after her. Presumably because some people outside the British Isles may not know who Elizabeth of Glamis is (or that Glamis is pronounced *Glarms*) the name was changed to Irish Beauty for the USA. Under any name it is one of the loveliest roses, with medium-sized clusters of large (4 in) double flowers in a beautiful soft salmon colour, somewhat deeper in the autumn. It has won top awards both as a rose itself, and separately for its fragrance, which is quite an achievement for a Floribunda. The plant is vigorous and bushy, with very free bloom and a quick repeat, carrying on until the frosts. There are, however, one or two possible drawbacks. In some districts its health is suspect, and some growers say that it does not transplant well. In fact there are nurseries which do not stock it for this reason; but certainly it does move quite happily from the nursery to the garden in most cases, and it may simply be that some types of soil do not suit it. It certainly gives little trouble on light, sandy soil, and all in all is a rose worth taking a chance with.

22 Fragrant Cloud (Duftwolke) Hybrid Tea. Also known as Nuage Parfumé. Tantau, 1963. Seedling × Prima Ballerina. This rose is considered by many to be the best Hybrid Tea produced since Peace. The large, full blooms are produced in incredible profusion, and tend to come in clusters. These should be at least partially disbudded to obtain the maximum size. Their shape is always good, with a high, firm centre in the early stages. Strong fragrance; the colour is a vivid geranium lake, which dulls a little with age. The leaves are large, glossy and dark green. Generally it is very healthy and stands wet weather well.

23 Pink Parfait Floribunda-Hybrid Tea type, or Grandiflora. Swim, 1960. First Love × Pinocchio. A very good rose in one of the quieter colourings that are so useful when one wishes to separate the stronger-coloured roses in a bedding scheme. The flowers are of medium to light pink, yellow at the base of the petals, and with an apricot reverse. They are quite large and of a good shape, though they eventually open flat. There is a slight fragrance, and the 2 ft 6 in to 3 ft bush is well branched and very free-flowering with, as a rule, medium-sized trusses. The leaves are mid-green and glossy. A good all-weather rose and also quite healthy.

24 My Girl (Curiosa) Floribunda. De Ruiter, 1964. Dacapo × Seedling. Large clusters of very double, cupped, deep salmon blooms distinguish this rose, in which the weight of the trusses may weigh down the rather slender canes and cause the plant to sprawl. It is a vigorous grower nonetheless, and has dark green, coppery foliage which may suffer from black spot.

25 Blue Moon (Also Mainzer Fastnacht or Sisi) Hybrid Tea. Tantau, 1964. Unknown seedling × Sterling Silver. A large, well-shaped double bloom of mauve – lavender colour, which is very fragrant. The bush is robust and upright, usually reaching 3 ft high, and it has large, deep green leaves which are generally healthy but will need watching for black spot in a bad year. However, it does tend to be of rather uneven growth and not to send up many new strong growths from the base of the plant.

26

26 Ernest H. Morse Hybrid Tea. Kordes, 1964. Parentage unknown. Ernest H. Morse has established itself as a strongly fragrant, bright, turkey-red rose of good form and size, which can produce exhibition quality blooms but is equally good for garden display. It seems to flower almost without ceasing, and although its many blooms lose their first bright glow rather quickly, they are still attractive. Growth is very robust, upright but bushing out well, and probably reaching 3 ft. Very good, large, semi-glossy dark green foliage, which rarely suffers from disease. It does not mind rain.

27 Chrysler Imperial Hybrid Tea. Lammerts, 1952. Charlotte Armstrong × Mirandy. One of the best red roses ever raised and, despite the fact that it is over twenty years old, still worth growing. The blooms are large, high-centred, and keep their shape well. They are crimson-red with darker shadings, but have one drawback that is common to so many roses of this colour; they blue with age and become much less attractive. Regular dead-heading would, of course, get rid of this problem. One other characteristic – this time a good one – that Chrysler Imperial has in common with most other reds is that it has a strong, sweet, fragrance. Growth is robust and upright to about 3 ft, and the large leaves are a matt, dark green. They should be watched for mildew. A number of good, dark red roses have been bred from this variety, including one of the best modern ones, Mister Lincoln.

28 First Love Hybrid Tea. Swim, 1952. Charlotte Armstrong × Show Girl. Yet another American rose bred from the prolific Charlotte Armstrong. This one has medium-sized blooms of 25 to 30 petals, which are pale pink with deeper shadings, and which last particularly well if cut for the house. They are fragrant and grow on a bushy plant, that spreads out well and will reach 3 ft. Mid-green, semi-glossy foliage. A good rose for bedding.

29 Manitou Hybrid Tea. Swim, 1957. Parentage unknown. A rose that would be more popular if it were more prolific with its blooms, for when they do come they are very large and very lovely, opening cupped and with plenty of petals, resembling deep coppery pink peonies. However, it is rare to get more than four or five on the plant at any one time, and there is a fairly long gap between the first and second flushes. The bush is vigorous and spreading and has deep green semi-glossy foliage. Not noticeably scented, but stands rain well.

30 Coral Queen Elizabeth Floribunda or Grandiflora. Gregory, 1966. Queen Elizabeth × unknown. There is clearly some doubt about the origin of this rose. Its official pedigree indicates that it comes from Queen Elizabeth, crossed with something else, as does Scarlet Queen Elizabeth, but in habit it looks like a sport on the line of White and Yellow Queen Elizabeth. Certainly it has its known parent's vigour and is a tall, robust grower, free-flowering, the blooms coming singly and in clusters. They are of a deep, coral pink, double and about 3 ins across, opening cupped. They are also fragrant.

28 29

31 Coralita Climber. Zombory, 1964. (New Dawn × Geranium Red) × Fashion. A short climber, or it can be grown as a shrub, for it will not go much over 6 ft. The dark red buds open to large, very double orange-coral flowers, which are borne extremely freely. Good, dark, leathery leaves. A useful rose for a pillar.

34

32 Maria Floribunda. Gregory, 1965. Unknown seedling × Border Beauty. The flowers of this rose are large for a Floribunda, being something like 3 ins across, and semi-double. They form large trusses, on which the flowers are well-spaced, only slightly fragrant, and of a very bright orange-scarlet. The strong-growing upright plant has dark, glossy leaves. Very free with its blooms, this was one of a number of sound, if not outstanding, Floribundas in the scarlet shades that did not quite reach the top of the sales charts.

33 Paprika Floribunda. Tantau, 1958. Märchenland × Red Favourite. Paprika was one of the early ones of the same batch as the previous rose, and it did make the grade, due not only to the fact that the competition at that time was not quite so fierce, but also because it was simply a very good rose. The flowers are even larger than those of Maria, semi-double, turkey-red and borne in enormous trusses. Growth is strong and the plant branches out well. It has plenty of glossy, olive green leaves; good in all weathers.

34 Wendy Cussons Hybrid Tea. Gregory, 1963. Independence × Eden Rose. Three Gold medals for this one, and it deserves them all, for it is very nearly the perfect garden rose and one that is equally good for exhibition. It is scarcely ever out of flower and carries masses of large, perfectly formed, high-centred blooms which seem to be impervious to rain. These are of a bright cerise-pink, and are also marvellously fragrant and will keep on coming until well into the autumn. The plant is on the tall side, but it branches out well and has glossy, dark green leaves with a hint of red about them. It is not quite proof against mildew, but generally healthy.

35

36

35 Strawberry Fair Floribunda. Gregory, 1966. Orangeade × unknown seedling. Very vigorous and bushy with dark green foliage which sets off well the trusses of scarlet, double flowers. These are of medium size (about 2 ins) and are slightly fragrant. Very free bloom and quite a good repeat.

36 Evelyn Fison (Irish Wonder in the USA) McGredy, 1961. Moulin Rouge × Korona. Yet another of the vast number of scarlet and orange-scarlet Floribundas. This one, however, has been outstanding, mainly because the bright scarlet, 2 in flowers seem to be virtually indestructible. Quite unfading in even the strongest sunshine, their short, tough petals enable them to stand up equally well to heavy and prolonged rain. They come in trusses which are usually medium-sized, though several times a year the bush is likely to send up truly enormous ones; the size of these, combined with the lasting power of the flowers when cut, make this a favourite rose in the Floribunda classes at shows. They have only slight fragrance. The bush is compact and spreads out well, growing to about 2 ft 6 ins, with mid- to light green very glossy leaves, which are normally very healthy. Evelyn Fison will flower well into the autumn and has a good repeat.

37 Lancastrian Hybrid Tea. Gregory, 1965. Ena Harkness × seedling. A very fragrant, crimson-scarlet and well-shaped rose, growing on a strong, upright bush. The leaves are light green and glossy, with sometimes a tint of crimson. This rose is a good one which seems to have been rather over-shadowed by others of the same colouring which were introduced at about the same time. It is particularly good in the autumn, but a tendency to mildew is a disadvantage.

38 Baccara Hybrid Tea. Meilland, 1956. Happiness × Independence. A rose that has more petals than almost any other, ranging in total between 72 and 82. They are, however, quite short, so that the globular bud opens well and the flowers as they develop are first cup-shaped and finally flat. As they last extremely well in water and have good long stems, this rose has for long been grown very extensively under glass for the cut flower trade. If you buy bright geranium-red roses at a florist, as likely as not you will be getting Baccara. In fact it is probably a better rose for this purpose than for the garden, at least in a damp climate. It was bred in the heat of the south of France. It is a strong and upright grower to about 3 ft, which is on the tall side for bedding in in modern small gardens. The foliage is dark and leathery.

39 Champs-Elysées Hybrid Tea. Meilland, 1957. Monique × Happiness. A good bedding rose that has been around some time, and has probably not been grown as widely as its qualities deserve. It will make a first-rate, colourful display, its large, cupped, crimson-red double flowers, coming in great profusion and repeating well and quickly, though they are only slightly fragrant. It forms a strong, upright bush to 2 ft 6 ins or 3 ft with good foliage.

39

40 Christian Dior Hybrid Tea. Meilland, 1961. (Sondermeldung × Happiness) × (Peace × Happiness). At its best a good rose for exhibitors, for the blooms come mainly one to a stem and are large, full, and high-centred. The inside of the petals is a beautiful velvety scarlet, with a rather duller scarlet on the reverse, but there is only slight fragrance. Growth is strong and upright, rarely exceeding 2 ft 6 ins. Will want watching for mildew and black spot.

40

41

42

41 Lilli Marlene Floribunda. Kordes, 1959. (Our Princess × Rudolph Timm) × Ama. Large, semi-double, crimson-scarlet flowers on large trusses, with however, only slight scent. The strong, well-branched plant, which will grow to 2 ft 6 ins, has matt, medium- to dark green foliage which often has bronze tints; the stems are plum-coloured when young. Good in the rain but may suffer from mildew. This rose should not be confused with Marlene, another Floribunda from the same raiser. The latter has noticeably smaller leaves and smaller flowers of a brighter red, and is much shorter in growth. It is an excellent dwarf rose for small beds or for edging larger ones.

42 Finale (Also Ami des Jardins). Floribunda, Kordes, 1964. A low-growing compact rose, useful for the small bed and small garden. The flowers, which come in good-sized clusters, are quite large, double, and of an attractive salmon-rose. Little scent but good weather resistance. Light green, generally healthy foliage.

43 Uncle Walter Hybrid Tea. McGredy, 1963. Detroiter × Heidelberg. No doubt because of one of its parents, Heidelberg, which is classified as a Floribunda-Shrub, is a very tall-growing rose which is often used in the shrub border itself. It is too tall and probably too ungainly in growth for bedding. It will reach at least 5 ft, but the canes, though naturally upright, can be weighed down by the weight of bloom, which comes very freely. Probably it is best to put it at the back of the border or amongst other shrub roses so that it has something to lean on, and where its rather untidy habit of growth is concealed. The blooms are lovely, large, double, crimson-scarlet, and of a good, high-centred form, though they are only slightly fragrant. The foliage, which can be sparse lower down, is of a good, glossy dark green and leathery in texture. It is not proof against mildew.

44 Orange Sensation Floribunda. De Ruiter, 1960. Parentage unknown. One of the best and gayest bedding roses so far produced, particularly so in its colour range; it is orange, shading to light vermilion at the petal edges. The latter colour intensifies as the flower ages. The blooming is extremely prolific and the flowers come on large trusses, of which there seem to be an endless succession. The flowers themselves are medium-sized, with a pointed centre at first and then opening slightly cupped and sweetly fragrant. Prolonged rain can stain the petal edges a rather unattractive red, but generally this rose stands up to bad weather as well as most, and showers will not affect it. Its habit of growth is very vigorous, spreading wide, so that it may be advisable to plant the bushes farther apart than usual, say at 2 ft intervals. It will rarely exceed 2 ft 6 ins in height. The leaves are matt, medium green and very plentiful, but are not proof against black spot and mildew, at least on light soils; the mildew particularly attacks the stalks of the flowers unless spraying is carried out. On better soils this tendency is not so apparent, but in any case it is a rose that is well worth a little extra trouble.

43

44

45

45 Orangeade Floribunda. McGredy, 1959.
Orange Sweetheart × Independence. Large, 3 in,
semi-double flowers of a glowing bright vermilion-
orange, which take on a deeper tone and lose a
little of their brilliance with age. They open quite
flat and have only slight fragrance. The well-
spaced trusses are of varying sizes but some can be
enormous, and they are very good for exhibiting as
they last well when cut, like most Floribundas. The
growth is very robust with good, strong canes,
upright but well branched out so that the flowers do
not come just at the top of the plant. The leaves are
very dark green and semi-glossy but, as with the
majority of orange roses, they are likely to need
spraying against black spot. This is because they
are all reasonably closely descended from a species
of Persian rose which was particularly prone to the
disease and which has handed the tendency on to
its offspring and their descendants. Nevertheless,
Orangeade is a very good rose indeed, repeating
well and fast, and will make a spectacular bed. A
climbing sport is also available.

46

46 Spanish Orange Floribunda. Gregory, 1966. Parentage unknown. Not a very well-known or widely grown rose, though there would still seem to be time for it to catch the public's fancy, as it is comparatively new. It is surprising how long it can sometimes take for a good rose to make its mark. That first-rate Hybrid Tea, Prima Ballerina, for instance, was introduced in 1958 and is only now beginning to be widely grown. In this case it was a question of sheer merit, plus the fact that it is one of the most strongly scented of modern roses, that gradually gained Prima Ballerina its recognition; but Spanish Orange may not be a rose of quite such outstanding quality. As its name implies, it comes in the orange range of colours with freely blooming trusses of small (1½ ins) very double flowers, which do rather resemble oranges. They have some fragrance and appear on a strong-growing but not very large bush, with dark, glossy leaves.

47 Beauté Hybrid Tea. Mallerin, 1954. Mme. Joseph Perraud × unnamed seedling. The flowers of this rose do not have a great many petals, which tends to make them open quickly. They are, however, of a lovely blend of orange-yellow and apricot and are beautiful in all their stages, from the long, tapering buds to the fully open blooms, which last a long time on the plant and are quite proof against rain. Only slight fragrance, but great profusion of bloom, which will carry on well into the autumn. The leaves make a good framework for the flowers, being dark green and semi-glossy. Black spot should be watched for. The plant is quite vigorous, branches out well, though it can be rather spindly. Up to 2 ft 6 ins in height.

48 Chinatown Floribunda, though sometimes classed as a shrub rose. Poulsen, 1963. Columbine × Clare Grammerstorf. This is one that will certainly go up to 4 ft if not 5 ft, but it bushes out well and can make a handsome specimen shrub. Its strong canes need no support and are clothed almost down to the ground with large, attractive, glossy, light green leaves, which are usually proof against disease. Normally it will bear many trusses of up to seven or eight 4 in, very double yellow flowers, the colour intensifying toward the centre of the bloom and with sometimes a touch of pink on the petal edges. The second flowering is not as profuse as the first and there will not be a great many blooms in between. From this point of view it behaves more like a Hybrid Tea than a Floribunda.

49 Raymón Bach Hybrid Tea. Dot, 1938. Luis Brinas × Condesa de Sástago. A Spanish rose that is not seen much nowadays and which has large and very double (probably 80 petals), rather globular, blooms. They are strongly fragrant and of a bright orange, which pales a little towards the petal edges. A robust grower with glossy, dark green foliage.

52

50 Vienna Charm Also known as Wiener Charme.
Hybrid Tea. Kordes, 1963. It has not been possible so far to
breed a robust and healthy rose in a deep, coppery orange, but
as this colour happens at the moment to be a great favourite
with the rose-growing public, breeders keep trying. It was
thought at first that the German breeder, Kordes, had
succeeded when he produced Vienna Charm, which has the
most magnificent, high-centred, fragrant flowers, good
enough for showing when at their best. But the plant on
which they grow once more turned out a disappointment. It is
vigorous enough, but tends to be rather uneven in habit, with
the likelihood that it will send up single, enormously long
shoots, well above the rest. This makes it look untidy and so
not really very suitable for bedding, where uniformity of
growth is usually wanted. However, this fault would not be
too serious for such an attractive rose if it were not for the
tendency of the canes to die back in any but the very mildest
of winters, often right to the base, so that one loses them all
together. In fact it is not uncommon for the plant to be killed.

51 Cover Girl Hybrid Tea. Von Abrams, 1960. Sutter's
Gold × (Mme. Henri Guillot × Seedling). The long, pointed
buds open into 5 in, double, high-centred flowers. They are in
blends of light orange, copper and gold and slightly scented,
and come in great profusion on an upright, bushy plant with
glossy, dark green leaves.

52 Dr. A. J. Verhage Hybrid Tea. Verbeek, 1960. Tawny
Gold × Baccara seedling. A most attractive golden yellow
rose, the colour deepening towards the centres of the
medium-sized double flowers. The edges of the petals are
pleasingly scalloped, which gives them a 'different' look, and
they are scented. This rose is generally considered to be best
under glass and it is widely used in the cut flower trade as its
blooms, apart from generally coming singly to a stem and
being produced very freely, last a long time when cut. But
it will do very well in the garden, where it forms a smallish
but reasonably vigorous bush with small, dark green, glossy
leaves that seem to be very healthy.

53 Amarillo Hybrid Tea. Von Abrams, 1961. Buccaneer ×
Lowell Thomas. Exceptionally fragrant for a yellow rose,
this one has large, high-centred blooms of rich gold on strong
flower stems. It is vigorous, upright, and free of bloom,
reaching 2 ft 6 ins to 3 ft. The leaves are leathery and light
green. Not too quick with its repeat flowering.

54

54 Golden Treasure Floribunda. Tantau, 1965. Parentage unknown. Deep yellow double blooms on good trusses make this a colourful, cheerful rose, though the yellow does fade after a time as with most Floribundas of this colour. The flowers are fairly large, up to 2½ ins, shapely in the early stages, and have a slight scent. Tall, strong growth and glossy, dark green leaves.

55 Buccaneer Unusual, in that it is known as a Hybrid Tea in Europe, but as a Grandiflora in America, which just goes to show how confusing the classification of roses can be. Swim, 1952. Golden Rapture × (Max Krause × Capt. Thomas). Buccaneer belongs to the group of very tall yellow roses, which includes Golden Giant and Gold Crown, all of which are too lanky to grow other than at the back of a border. Buccaneer is more prolific with its blooms than the others. They are of medium size, buttercup yellow, and cupped in shape when fully open. They have only a slight fragrance. The growth is vigorous and upright, probably to at least 4 ft, and the leaves are matt green.

56 Arthur Bell Floribunda. McGredy 1965. Clare Grammerstorf × Piccadilly. One of the better yellow Floribundas, though no-one has produced a perfect one yet. All, with the exception of Allgold, which tends to be irregular in growth, fade to creamy yellow in strong sunlight, and Arthur Bell is certainly not proof against this failing. However, its large, full flowers, golden yellow at first, are still attractive when they turn to cream, and have the advantage that they are extremely fragrant. Good, mid-green foliage on an upright grower above the average in height, probably going up to 3 ft.

57 King's Ransom Hybrid Tea. Morey, 1961. Golden Masterpiece × Lydia. Undoubtedly the best pure yellow Hybrid Tea for general garden use as it is much more compact in growth than most and is unlikely to top 3 ft. The flowers are not over-large, but are of a good shape, with the outer petals reflexing nicely. They are borne freely with a quick repeat, though they are only slightly scented. The dark green, plentiful foliage may suffer from mildew.

58 Mary Poppins Hybrid Tea. Lens, 1965. Belle Etoile × (Michele Meilland × Tawny Gold). Also known as Lady Sunshine and not to be confused with another Hybrid Tea called Mary Poppins, which is shell-pink and was raised in the USA by Morey in 1967. One of the few yellow roses with a true rose perfume. Of medium height, it would be good for bedding if it had more flowers at any one time. When they do come, they are very large and of a good form. Mid-green leaves which may get black spot.

59

60

59 Golden Jewel Also known as Bijou d'Or and Goldjuwel. Floribunda. Tantau, 1959. Goldilocks × Masquerade seedling. There is little doubt that this would be one of the best yellow Floribundas of all if only it were more continuously in flower or even if, after a longish rest in the middle of the summer, its second flush of bloom were better. In its first flowering it is magnificent, with trusses of up to ten very double, bright yellow, fragrant flowers like 3 in pompons. They last on the bush a very long time and the individual flowers stand up to rain well. However, they are rather close together, and if one that is fading should get wet the petals can be prevented from falling cleanly and can spoil the buds forming underneath. It is as well to shake them out. The foliage is dark and glossy and very healthy. The bush will grow vigorously to about 2 ft 6 ins, branching well.

60 Norris Pratt There seems to be some doubt as to whether this is classed as a Hybrid Tea or a Floribunda. Buisman, 1967. Mrs. Pierre S. du Pont × Marcelle Gret. Both these parent roses are Hybrid Teas, which should make it a Hybrid Tea as well, but its United Kingdom introducer describes it as a Floribunda, perhaps because its tendency is to flower in clusters with great profusion. The deep yellow, unfading blooms are of classic Hybrid Tea shape, large, and grow on a bush of moderate vigour. Leaves dark and leathery.

61 Bossa Nova Hybrid Tea. McGredy, 1964. Leverkusen × Buccaneer. Big, 4 in, double blooms in a strong golden yellow that seems to be quite unfading. Large, glossy foliage on a vigorous plant which is rather above average height. Healthy, but not over-generous with its flowers between the two main flushes, though it is reasonably free during them. Watch for black spot.

62 Baby Masquerade Miniature. Also known as Baby Carnaval. Tantau, 1956. Tom Thumb × Masquerade. While this is a true miniature rose, one of its parents is the Floribunda Masquerade, and it is very like it in many ways on a small scale. It is one of the tallest of the miniatures and will make a very bushy plant (which is likely to need a lot of thinning out at pruning time) reaching as much as 15 ins in height, while the average for miniatures is about 9 ins. The flowers come in trusses as on the parent variety, opening from ovoid buds; they are chrome yellow at first, passing through pink to rose red, all colours being on the truss at one time as the blooms open in succession. Coming very early into flower, Baby Masquerade almost always has some bloom showing, right through into the autumn, and will make a good edging for a bed of larger roses. Because of its size it is less likely to be swamped by them as some of the other, smaller, miniatures may be. And, flowering early, it will give some colour before the other full-sized roses are out. It needs to be watched for mildew.

63 Simple Simon Miniature. de Vink, 1955. (*Rosa multiflora nana* × Mrs Pierre S. du Pont) × Tom Thumb. This is one of the smaller of the miniatures, not over 6 ins tall, but it is one of the best, giving little trouble. During its long flowering period it is covered in clusters of tiny blooms of carmine-rose, which have a yellow tinge at the petal bases. The flowers are double and the foliage glossy.

64 Coralin (Carolin, Carolyn or Karolyn). Miniature. Dot, 1955. Méphisto × Perla de Alcanada. Coral pink blooms, large, and of Hybrid Tea shape. They grow very freely on a low, bushy and compact plant which will reach 8 ins. One of the most attractive of the miniatures.

63

64

Miniature roses, of which a selection is shown on the preceding page, these two pages, and the two that follow, are miniatures in the full sense. They are not just rose bushes with small flowers, but the size of the plant, the leaves and the flowers are all in perfect scale. It is possible nowadays to obtain miniature standard or tree roses, and miniature climbers as well. They all have the same requirements as their larger cousins, and also some of the same weaknesses; they, too, can get mildew and black spot and be attacked by aphis or greenfly. But they have the charm of anything that is tiny and neat. Pruning will probably have to be done with nail scissors and consists of cutting out over-crowded growth and any dead wood, and the tipping back of the other shoots.

65 Yellow Doll Miniature. Moore, 1962. Golden Glow × Zee. Quite a tall one, which will reach 12 ins. The pointed buds open to fine, Hybrid Tea-shaped flowers, very double and with 50 to 60 petals, fragrant, and of a good, deep yellow. The leaves are dark green and glossy. Though tall, it is also bushy.

66 Little Flirt Miniature. Moore, 1961. *Rosa wichuraiana* × Floradora. A cross between a species rambler and a Floribunda, it is difficult to see how this ended up a miniature, but it did – and a good one too. The blooms are fragrant, bright orange-red, and with a yellow reverse to the petals, giving a very gay effect. Masses of bloom on a bushy plant that will reach 9 to 10 ins, and which has light green leaves.

65

66

67

67 Baby Darling Miniature. Moore, 1964. Little Darling × Magic Wand. Small, double flowers of about 20 petals of an orange-pink. Dwarf, bushy growth to about 10 ins. A descendant of the Gold Medal winner, Little Darling, and inheriting many of its good qualities.

68 June Time Miniature. Moore, 1963. (*Rosa wichuraiana* × Floradora) × (Etoile Luisante seedling × Red Ripples). Half the parentage is the same as Little Flirt, but the result is very different. The small, many-petalled flowers are light pink with a deeper reverse. They grow in clusters on a bushy, compact, 10 in plant, which has glossy, mid-green leaves.

69 New Penny Miniature. Moore, 1962. (*Rosa wichuraiana* × Floradora) × unnamed seedling. Once again some of the same parents have produced a different result. The flowers are only semi-double, small, scented and of a strong orange-pink. Plenty of them on a good bushy grower with shiny leaves, that will reach 9 to 10 in.

70 Eleanor Miniature. Moore, 1960. (*Rosa wichuraiana* × Floradora) × (Seedling × Zee). Very small and very double flowers, opening from slim, pointed buds to a coral-pink which deepens as the flower ages. A good, free bloomer that will go up to 12 ins and has leathery, glossy leaves.

68

Miniature roses are often sold in pots and the implication is that they are good house-plants. This is only partially true, as they will not do well if they are kept in the house all the time, especially in the dry atmosphere of central heating. For the best results they should be kept out of doors until they are just coming into bloom and, when the flowers are over, taken outside again until the next flowering. They are perfectly hardy and can safely be left out of doors all winter, though in extreme climates they will need winter protection, like other roses. The pots should be plunged in the soil and watered if they dry out. The best way to grow miniature roses is in a rockery garden (provided that they have a deep, cool root run), in stone troughs on a terrace, or as edgings to a bed of larger roses. It is also possible to make a complete miniature rose garden with them, which will need either extremely fine grass or paving between the beds. Ordinary grass can overwhelm the tiny roses.

69

70

71 Fire King Floribunda. Meilland, 1958. Moulin Rouge × Fashion. Full, very double fiery scarlet blooms in large trusses. The flowers eventually open flat and are scented, and are carried on the plant until well into the autumn. The leaves are dark green and the rose is a very strong-growing one, upright but bushy. This rose was a worthy All-American Winner in 1960, and originated in France.

72 Circus Floribunda. Swim, 1956. Fandango × Pinocchio. Also an All-American Winner, with several Gold Medals to its name as well, this is a rose that has been popular everywhere – and deservedly so. It is one of the best of all Floribundas and gives a tremendous show of flowers over a very long period, repeating remarkably quickly. The blooms are probably up to 3 ins across, very double, and are carried on large trusses, opening cupped. They are scented (though not very strongly) and open bright yellow, shaded with pink and salmon. Gradually the colours merge to a delicate apricot-orange. They are just about rain-proof and will open in the dullest weather. The healthy, bushy plant will reach 2 ft 6 ins.

73 Modern Times Hybrid Tea. Verbeek, 1956. A sport from Red Better Times. A great many of the old shrub roses are striped pink and white, particularly among the *gallicas*. As these figure largely in the parentage of modern roses it is rather surprising that there are not more Hybrid Teas or Floribundas in this very attractive combination. Those that are striped (not invariably in pink and white) have all been sports, so one of their ancestors is probably making its presence felt. Modern Times is such a rose, red, striped pale pink to white, and fragrant. It has profuse bloom which grows on a robust plant with light green foliage, which may get mildew. Unfortunately the colours, though bright and contrasting well when the flower first opens, tend to fade somewhat rapidly, so that the overall effect is very soon that of a pale pink rose.

74 Bajazzo Hybrid Tea. Kordes, 1961. Parentage unknown. A strong-growing Hybrid Tea with large, well-shaped and very fragrant blooms of a velvety texture, deep red and with a white reverse to the petals. An upright plant with mid-green foliage, it could be more free with its blooms in between the two main flushes.

72

73   74

75 **Charleston** Floribunda. Meilland, 1963. Masquerade × (Radar × Caprice). If you live in an area where black spot and mildew are prevalent, do not read any further, because Charleston is particularly prone to both. In other respects it can be recommended as a very vigorous grower to about 3 ft, with dark green, glossy foliage and very showy blooms. They are large, on good-sized trusses, and of a startlingly bright yellow, flushed crimson. Unlike its parent, Masquerade, the colours do not change or merge into each other, and in every respect except that of health it is a more attractive rose.

76　77

76　Doreen　Hybrid Tea. Robinson, 1951. Lydia ×
McGredy's Sunset. It is always difficult to tell why some
roses of great merit still do not become widely planted.
Doreen has never received the acclaim it deserves, for it
is a first-rate, low-growing bedding rose, which will
flower right through the season and seems not to mind
damp and cold. The flowers are large and of a beautiful
shape with the high, pointed centres of the classic bloom,
and many are of exhibition standard. They are a deep
golden orange, with scarlet flushes, growing on a
spreading, bushy plant with dark green, glossy leaves.
It is remarkably healthy for a rose in this colour range.

77　Summer Rainbow　Hybrid Tea. Jelly, 1966. Peace ×
Dawn. Large, double, high-centred blooms which are
slightly fragrant. They are pink, with the reverse of the
petals yellow, and make a striking bed. Free blooms
grow on a strong, bushy plant which has dark green,
glossy foliage. The rose is not too well known and has
still to make a name for itself.

78　Piccadilly　Hybrid Tea. McGredy, 1959. McGredy's
Yellow × Karl Herbst. This is just about the best rose to
have come from that well-known Irish breeder, McGredy.
One parent was the best yellow rose of its time, and the
other, Karl Herbst, was used so often as a parent in
breeding roses that it became known in the rose world as
'The Bull'. Piccadilly is a vigorous, upright grower to
2 ft 6 ins, with very handsome, healthy foliage, changing
from bronze when young to a good, glossy dark green.
The large, high-centred flowers are bright red, with an
equally bright yellow reverse to the petals. As the blooms
age, however, the colours gradually merge and the whole
bloom becomes suffused with a marvellous mixture of red,
gold and orange tones. A showy rose, and certainly the
best bi-colour amongst the red and yellow combinations.
It can get both mildew and black spot, but rarely badly.
Only very slight fragrance, but almost always in bloom,
weather-proof, and particularly good in the autumn.

78

79 Westminster Hybrid Tea. Robinson, 1960. Gay Crusader × Peace. This rose won a Gold Medal, but it is rather doubtful now whether it should have, as it has a good many weaknesses. The large, double blooms are attractive when newly opened and are cherry-red with a yellow reverse, but they soon lose their shape and the colours fade. And, surprisingly for a rose with comparatively few petals, it does not open particularly well in wet weather, and is a poor performer in the autumn. It is a tall and lanky grower with not many leaves lower down. The foliage is semi-glossy and mid-green, with bronze tints. On the other hand, it is extremely fragrant.

80 Stella Hybrid Tea, or Grandiflora. Tantau, 1958. Horstmann's Jubiläumsrose × Peace. However you like to classify it, this is one of the loveliest roses ever raised. It has huge, 5 in, high-centred blooms, creamy-white in the centre, flushed pink and deepening to carmine at the petal edges, with the carmine becoming blush pink in the late season's flowers. A winner at many shows. The flowers repeat quickly, although they tend to come in clusters and to be rather smaller in the autumn; this can be stopped by disbudding. They are completely rain-proof, but only slightly scented. An extremely strong and upright grower, which will reach 3 ft, its healthy, dark, glossy leaves sometimes have a bronze tint. One of the small band of roses that is equally good for the garden and for exhibition.

81 Eden Rose Hybrid Tea. Meilland, 1950. Peace × Signora. One of the descendants of Peace which has inherited a lot of its parent's robustness, for it has strong, tall, branching growth, though unlike Peace, it will want watching for mildew. The flowers have a lot of petals and tend to be globular in form and to open quickly, though at their best they have a good shape and have been successful in shows. They have a strong fragrance and are deep pink with a silvery reverse. Glossy, dark green leaves with bronze tints. Not one of the newer roses, but still worth a place in the garden.

82

83

82 Lavendula Floribunda. Kordes, 1965. Magenta ×
Sterling Silver. A reasonably good, lavender-coloured
Floribunda, very free with its bloom but rather suspect from
the health point of view. Free, but not very robust growth,
made up for to some extent by its very large and fragrant
flowers, which grow in medium-sized trusses. As with most
roses in this colour they tend to fade in strong sunlight. Dark
green leaves. Watch for mildew.

83 Mojave Hybrid Tea. Swim, 1954. Charlotte Armstrong
× Signora. The name is pronounced *Mo-harv-ay* and the rose
was named after the Mojave Indians of North America.
It is a fine rose, even though it does have rather few petals
and in consequence opens quickly. It makes a very striking
display, for its colours are those of a sunset; burnt orange
and flame, prominently veined, with scented and medium
sized blooms. The plant is very tall-growing and erect, so
it is best in small groups at the back of a border, or for
bedding on its own in a fairly large bed. Very healthy and
particularly good late in the year, it has glossy, bronze-green
leaves.

84 Firebeam Floribunda. Fryer, 1960. Masquerade ×
Unknown seedling. 2½ in, semi-double, very strongly scented
flowers carried on good-sized trusses. Vigorous growth and
free bloom. The flowers are a rich blend of flame, yellow and
red, the colour holding well as the flower ages. Good, glossy
foliage; some black spot possible.

85 Anna Louisa Floribunda. De Ruiter, 1967. Highlight
× Valeta. Borne in medium-sized to large clusters, the soft
pink flowers are very full and quite delightful. A strong but
low-growing plant that bushes out well, it carries matt,
mid-green leaves which are usually healthy but may get
black spot. It does not mind rain at all. Quite a new
Floribunda, which should have a future if it fulfils its
present promise.

86 Geisha Girl Floribunda. McGredy, 1964. Gold Cup ×
McGredy's Yellow. One of the Floribundas that starts life as
a strong yellow, but fades to cream as the blooms age. The
flowers grow on well-spaced trusses, are about 3½ ins in
diameter, well-shaped at first, but open more or less flat and
rather formless. Tall, branching growth and large, medium-
green, matt leaves which are plentiful, unusually long and
pointed in shape. Very free with its flowers, and a good
repeat.

87 Colour Wonder (Königin der Rosen). Hybrid Tea.
Kordes, 1964. Parentage unknown. This is a short (2 ft),
compact grower with very thorny stems and shiny, olive-
green leaves. The flowers are very full, with good high
centres, fragrant and of a light nasturtium orange with a
yellow reverse to the petals. It is a most attractive combination
of colours, but unfortunately this rose is not very generous in
its blooming. If cut, the flowers last at least a week in water,
holding their shape perfectly.

88 Margot Fonteyn Hybrid Tea. McGredy, 1964.
Independence × Ma Perkins. 4 in double flowers of 40
petals, of a good shape and coming very freely on a
strong-growing bush. They are very fragrant and coloured
rich salmon-orange. Good, mid-green leaves, generally very
healthy.

89 Rose Gaujard Hybrid Tea. Gaujard, 1959. Peace ×
Opera seedling. A good beginner's rose as it is extremely
healthy and robust, and will grow almost anywhere with the
minimum of attention. It produces an abundance of bloom in
all weathers, the flowers being of exhibition shape and
quality when at their best, though there is a tendency for
them to come with split centres which does not matter too
much for garden display. They last a long time when cut, and
are pale pink to white, flushed and edged carmine, and with a
silvery reverse. Some fragrance, but it is not strong. The
growth, however, is strong and upright, but branching out
well, with good, glossy, dark green leaves.

86

87

88

89

90

91

90 Zambra Floribunda. Meilland, 1961. (Goldilocks × Fashion) × (Goldilocks × Fashion). This rose when it first comes out is one of the most attractive. Its blooms open flat, are semi-double, and are of the most lovely soft, coppery orange with a bright yellow reverse to the petals. Indeed it is the only rose in this particular colour combination, but unfortunately the blooms do not age very well and the petals do not fall cleanly. Instead they turn to a rather dirty pink and need shaking off the plant if the following display is not to be spoiled. As each flush lasts over a long period, and the flowers on the medium-sized trusses open in succession, it is very necessary to do this. The bush is low-growing to about 2 ft or a little more, and spreads out to 3 ft or so. It does, however, follow the pattern of orange roses in that its health is suspect, and black spot is a certainty unless the plant is sprayed. There can be some mildew, too, all of which is a great pity in a rose of unique colour. Slight fragrance only.

91 Wisbech Gold Hybrid Tea. McGredy, 1964. Piccadilly × Golden Sun. It is one of the curiosities of rose-breeding that two roses as tall as Piccadilly and Golden Sun should produce the very short Wisbech Gold, which may not exceed 2 ft. But it is a fact that, so mixed is their ancestry, if you cross two roses together you never know for certain what you are going to get. This cross produced an unexpected bonus, because short-growing roses are very much in demand and there are not all that many of them. Despite its low stature, Wisbech Gold is a vigorous and compact grower with good, dark green, glossy leaves. The flowers are large, opening cupped, but are only slightly scented. Golden yellow in colour, the petal edges are tinted cerise-pink. A profuse bloomer, but may need protection from mildew.

92 Masquerade Floribunda. Boerner, 1949. Goldilocks × Holiday. This rose really caught the attention of rose growers when it was first introduced, nearly 25 years ago. People had forgotten that it was quite usual for roses in Victorian times to change through several colours as they aged, and this is just what Masquerade does. None of the old ones were, however, in its particular colour combination. The medium-sized, semi-double flowers, carried on very large trusses, are bright yellow when they first open, turn to salmon-pink and then to a dark and not too attractive red. As the flowers open in succession, all these colours are present in the truss at one time, and it is this gay and very colourful effect that gave the rose its name. There is only very slight scent. The bush is very strong-growing and will generally reach 3 ft, branching out well.

94

95

96

93 Brasilia Hybrid Tea. McGredy, 1968. Perfecta × Piccadilly. Large, well-shaped blooms, bright scarlet with the reverse silvery white, tinted yellow. They can be as much as 4 ins across. A strong, upright grower with a fair show of flowers. Semi-glossy, medium green leaves; generally very healthy.

94 Princess Margaret of England Hybrid Tea. Meilland, 1968. Queen Elizabeth × (Peace × Michèle Meilland). Not to be confused with Princess Margaret Rose, which is also a pink Hybrid Tea and still in commerce, though not very widely distributed. The latter has small, beautifully shaped flowers on a small bush. Both plant and blooms of Princess Margaret of England are bigger, the flowers being moderately full and of a much stronger phlox pink. They only have a slight scent. Growth is robust, upright, and quite well branched. The leaves are a matt, leathery, light green.

95 Black Velvet Hybrid Tea. Morey, 1960. New Yorker × Happiness. Huge, 5 to 5½ in double flowers with high centres, very well scented and of a deep wine red. As often as not they come singly on good strong stems, which makes them good for cutting. Strong growth, free bloom, and leathery dark leaves. Watch out for mildew.

96 Pernille Poulsen Floribunda. Poulsen, 1965. Ma Perkins × Columbine. In many ways this resembles a low-growing and more compact Elizabeth of Glamis, though the salmon-pink has more pink in it and less salmon, and it does fade much lighter. Although fragrant, it has not the wonderful scent of the latter rose. The flowers are large, often 4 ins across, come very freely on small to medium trusses, and are amongst the first to appear in early summer. The branching bush is well covered in medium-green, semi-glossy leaves, which are unusually long and tapering. Mildew, again, is a possible hazard.

97 Golden Showers Climber. Lammerts, 1956. Charlotte Armstrong × Capt. Thomas.
Yet another offspring of Charlotte Armstrong, which has been the seed parent of so many
good American roses. This time it produced a rose that is more than just good, for it is one
of the few climbers that can truly be called perpetual-flowering. Starting early in the season
its long, pointed buds, showing orange at first, open into large, semi-double, fragrant and
rather loosely-formed flowers of a quite unfading daffodil yellow. They go on and on
blooming on long straight stems, often singly, so that they are good for cutting and last well
in water. Not one of the tallest climbers; it will certainly reach 7 or 8 ft, though in the right
spot it will go higher, its healthy and glossy dark green leaves clothing a wall or pillar well
and showing off the flowers to perfection. It can also be successfully grown, too, as a large
free shrub, needing only the minimum of support.

98 Border Coral Floribunda. De Ruiter, 1958. Signal Red × Fashion. A strong,
spreading rose of first-rate constitution that bears large trusses of 2½ to 3 in flowers of
coral-salmon, yellow tinted at the base of the petals and fragrant. It is very free-flowering
and has a good repeat performance. Large, glossy, mid-green leaves. Probably not much
above 2 ft in height. As an offspring of two roses not noted for their resistance to disease,
it is surprisingly healthy.

99 Sympathie Climber. Kordes, 1964. Parentage unknown. This German rose is one of a
very hardy race of climbers and robust shrubs that has been bred for toughness, standing up
well to the harsh winters often encountered in northern Europe. Many of them can be grown
either as short climbers, suitable for a pillar or low wall, or as large, loose-growing shrubs,
so that it is not uncommon to find them under either heading in nursery catalogues.
Sympathie is one of the taller ones and will reach 12 ft. It would make a very big shrub
indeed and would hardly be suitable for a small garden in this form. The flowers are very full,
fragrant, bright red and with a velvety texture to the petals. Glossy, mid-green leaves.

100 Etude Climber. Gregory, 1968. Danse du Feu (Spectacular) × The New Dawn. Flowering in clusters all along its vigorous lateral growths, Etude has good recurrent bloom and is a wall or pillar rose. The medium-sized, semi-double flowers are of a deep salmon-pink and only slightly scented. Very free, branching growth and rather small dark green glossy leaves.

101 Autumn Sunlight Climber. Gregory, 1965. Danse du Feu (Spectacular) × Cl. Goldilocks. Fragrant, rather globular flowers of a bright orange-vermilion. They are of medium size and double, with about 30 petals, and grow in clusters with great abandon. Very vigorous growth and glossy, bright green leaves.

102 Elegance Climber. Brownell, 1937. Glenn Dale × Mary Wallace seedling. It seems right to include one of the older climbers which has stood the test of time, particularly as Elegance has some of the loveliest flowers of any of this group; very large, high-centred, of classic Hybrid Tea form and exhibition standard. Many come singly on long stems, though later in the season they may be in small clusters of three or four and are likely to be rather smaller. They are a soft yellow, deepening towards the heart of the flower, but lack a strong scent, which would have made them perfect. This is not a perpetual-flowering rose, but starts to bloom early in June and will carry on well into July. It may possibly bear a few flowers later, but this is a rare occurrence and cannot be counted on. An enormously strong grower, it will reach 10 to 15 ft, with good light green foliage which may need watching for mildew on dry soils.

100

101   102

103 Pink Pérpetue Climber. Gregory, 1965. Danse du Feu (Spectacular) × The New Dawn. This rose has exactly the same parents as Etude, but there are quite a number of differences in the two roses. This one has blooms of clear pink with a carmine pink reverse, which grow in medium-sized clusters. It makes an excellent and very recurrent pillar rose, but though vigorous it does not grow very tall. Only slightly fragrant and with glossy, dark green, rather small leaves.

104 Albertine Barbier, 1921. *Rosa wichuraiana* × Mrs. Arthur Robert Waddell. This is a rose that is usually classified as a rambler, but occasionally you will see it called a climber. Really it seems to be half-way between the two. The flowers are on the large side for a rambler, and they grow just as freely on the old wood of the previous years as they do on the new canes, unlike most ramblers. In June, but not later on, it is literally smothered with its high-centred, medium-sized, coppery-pink blooms, whose scent can be detected from quite a distance. Eventually the flowers open rather loosely and the colour fades a little, but for sheer profusion there is not a rose to beat it. It is enormously vigorous, with rather stiff and thorny growth, and for this reason it is a little surprising that it is sold so often as a weeping standard or tree rose. The whole point of these latter varieties is that the canes should be very pliable and hang down to form a natural umbrella, trailing almost to the ground, as a rambler like Excelsa will do. Albertine will shoot off in all directions and takes considerable training if it is to achieve this effect, though mind you, the struggle is worth it in the end. It can, however, make a spectacular large shrub if you have plenty of space, but will probably need some support. The example in the picture is grown in this way. The semi-glossy, dark green leaves are tinted red when young and are not proof against mildew, though, unlike many of the old ramblers, it can quite easily be controlled by spraying.

106

107

105 Dortmund Kordes, 1955. Seedling × *Rosa kordesii*. Another of the hardy German Kordes roses which were mentioned when describing Sympathie (**99**). This one has very different flowers, single, large, and red with a very distinct white eye. They are very striking and are recurrent, growing in large clusters on a branching but only moderately vigorous plant, which will reach 8 ft as a pillar rose or else make a large specimen bush. The flowers are scented and the leaves dark and glossy.

106 Voie Lactée Climbing Hybrid Tea. Robichon, 1949. Frau Karl Druschki × Luien Pontin. Not very often seen outside its native France, but worth growing if you can obtain it. Coming from globular buds, the flowers open into large, double and very fragrant creamy-white blooms on a strong-growing climber with glossy foliage. Some mildew a possibility, probably inherited from one of its parents, Frau Karl Druschki, one of the most famous white roses of all time, but very prone to attack by disease.

107 Bantry Bay Climber. McGredy, 1967. The New Dawn × Korona. One of a new generation of McGredy climbers and an extremely promising one. The flowers are widely spaced in the trusses and are pink with a touch of salmon, deeper in the centre of the blooms. They are of medium size and semi-double, with slight fragrance. A very healthy rose, strong-growing, and with good, glossy mid-green leaves.

108

108 Parade Large-flowered Climber. Boerner, 1957. New Dawn Seedling × Cl. World's Fair. A good, vigorous, repeat-flowering climber, which will reach 10 ft in height and which has glossy, dark green foliage, tinted red. There is a long-lasting and very profuse first flush of bloom in June, some intermittent flowering after that, and then a second flush which is good but does not match the first. Suitable for a wall, fence or pergola, but a bit on the tall side for a pillar. The double flowers, which are only slightly fragrant, are a mixture of carmine and crimson. A good shape at first, they open rather loosely, showing golden stamens. They make a fine display.

There are a number of other good climbers that are worth trying, and nowadays there are far more that will flower more than once. For many years it was not considered commercially worthwhile to spend much time or trouble in breeding new varieties, as they were bought in comparatively small numbers. Consequently many of those still in the nursery lists have been going a long time, though only the best of the old ones have survived; and most of these only flower once.

In recent times, on both sides of the Atlantic, things have changed, and now there is a growing number of repeat-flowering climbers to choose from and some that are reasonably recurrent. A number of these have already been described, but here are brief details of a few more that are well worth growing.

Aloha has wonderful, very double, deep pink flowers, sweetly fragrant. It is not a very tall grower and can be used equally well as a shrub. It is quite disease-proof. Casino is a Gold Medal winner and has double, scented blooms of a soft yellow; it will grow up to 9 ft or so. Copenhagen, on the other hand, is bright scarlet. It is fragrant and, like Aloha, will make a good large shrub, as it does not grow much above 8 ft and bushes out well.

With Coral Dawn we are back to the pinks, the scented flowers opening cupped. About 10 ft is its maximum height. Crimson Shower is a rambler, and a comparatively modern one, dating from 1951. True ramblers do not repeat, but on this one the flowers last from July to September. It has the typical rambler clusters of small crimson semi-double flowers. With Danse du Feu, or Spectacular, to use its American name, we are back with the climbers. It is double, orange-scarlet, and has bronze-tinted foliage. There is a good repeat, but it should not be planted in hot, dry soils or bad mildew will be likely.

Handel dates from 1965 and has particularly lovely and unusual blooms, creamy white, flushed pink at the petal edges. Only slight fragrance, but strong growth to 10 or 12 ft. High Noon is a yellow with fragrant semi-double blooms, suitable for a pillar. Joseph's Coat is cherry-red and yellow; another pillar rose or shrub, and very eye-catching.

Extremely free with its flowers and recurrent, Parkdirektor Riggers has blood-red semi-double, 3 in blooms and vigorous growth. One of the best, despite its somewhat unattractive name, which indicates its German parentage. Rosy Mantle is one of the newest varieties and dates from 1968. It has moderately full, rose-pink flowers, borne in small clusters, and is covered with glossy, dark green foliage. Schoolgirl has an unusual colour for a climber, orange-apricot, and has large, very double and fragrant blooms. And finally, for those who like single roses, there is the crimson-scarlet Soldier Boy; the hips should be removed after the first flowering if a good repeat crop is wanted.